DATE

# to be now
## new and selected poems

# to be now

new and selected poems

1989-2003

marty gervais

mosaic press

National Library of Canada Cataloguing in Publication Data

Gervais, C. H. (Charles Henry), 1946-
    To be now : new & selected poems, 1989-2003 / Marty
Gervais.

ISBN 0-88962-802-5

                    I. Title.

PS8563.E7T6 2003        C811'.54        C2003-900351-5
PR9199.3.G45T6 2003

Published by Mosaic Press, offices and warehouse at 1252
Speers Road, Units 1 and 2, Oakville, Ontario, L6L 5N9, Canada
and Mosaic Press, PMB 145, 4500 Witmer Industrial Estates,
Niagara Falls, NY, 14305-1386, U.S.A.

Mosaic Press acknowledges the assistance of the Canada Council
and the Department of Canadian Heritage, Government of
Canada for their support of our publishing programme.

Le Conseil des Arts | The Canada Council
du Canada | for the Arts

Mosaic Press in Canada:
1252 Speers Road, Units 1 & 2,
Oakville, Ontario
L6L 5N9
Phone/Fax: 905-825-2130
mosaicpress@on.aibn.com

Mosaic Press in U.S.A.:
4500 Witmer Industrial Estates
PMB 145, Niagara Falls, NY
14305-1386
Phone/Fax: 1-800-387-8992
mosaicpress@on.aibn.com

www.mosaic-press.com

Other books by Marty Gervais

The Science of Nothing (2000)
Tearing Into A Summer Day (1996)
Playing God (1994)
Scenes from the Present (1991)
Autobiographies (1989)
Letters from the Equator (1986)
Into A Blue Morning (1982)
Up Country Lines (1979)
Poems for American Daughters (1976)

Photo by Dan Janisse/*Windsor Star*

# Acknowledgements

The author wishes to thank a number of individuals whose advice, encouragement and support helped make this book. These include Howard Aster, whose idea it was to put these poems together, and whose faith in my work put these works into print for the first time; John B. Lee, who did the initial editing and selection, and made me rethink and reshape much of these poems; Robert Hilles who read most of these over the years, and told me where I messed up; and Roger Bell, Bob Hill, Greg Gatenby, Paul Vasey, Karen Mulhallen, and so many others. Thanks must also go to Descant for first giving exposure to these poems. I am most grateful to the monks at Gethsemani, especially to Rev. Timothy Kelly and Brother Paul Quenon for making it possible to find that space and time to write in silence. Finally, I must thank my wife, Donna, for her patience and faith.

Many poems in the first section, God's Lies, have appeared in the following anthologies: *Larger Than Life, Earth Songs, Following The Plough, Smaller Than God* and *Body Language*. Other poems appeared in the following magazines: *Descant, Literary Review of Canada* and *The Windsor Review*.

The poems in the second section are from: *The Science of Nothing* (2000, Mosaic Press), *Tearing Into A Summer Day* (1996, Mosaic Press), *Playing God* (1994, Mosaic Press), and *Scenes from the Present* (1991, Penumbra Press) and Autobiographies (1989, Penumbra Press).

# Table of Contents

Introduction

*One*. God's Lies / 1
      New Poems

# Making A Difference
## By John B. Lee

A few years ago, Marty Gervais, Roger Bell and I
were driving through a relatively poor district of
Montavello, Alabama when Marty spotted a man lean-
ing against the porch railing of a small home reading a
book. "Stop here," said Marty. "I want to photograph
that man." We pulled into the parking lot of a Baptist
church across the road and waited while Marty crossed
over and began to engage the fellow in conversation.
We couldn't hear a word from our vantage, but we
witnessed from that distance how Marty engaged the
man in conversation as if the two were lifelong friends.
The stranger gestured and invited Marty up onto his
porch and before long began posing as Marty photo-
graphed him leaning on the railing, sitting on the old
porch swing, and gazing out over his lawn. What had
Marty said to put the man at ease; to make him so obvi-
ously comfortable, familiar and compliant? An hour, ten
photographs and perhaps two poems later, Marty re-
turned to rejoin Roger and me on our journey. As we
pulled away, the man waved as if he were wishing
farewell to an old pal. "What did you say to that man?"
I asked. "I told him I had a porch swing like that as a
child." It couldn't possibly be that simple. Indeed, the
man had told Marty his life story. How he'd been poor
all his life. How he aspired to improve his lot. How the
book he was reading would help. What plans he had for
the future. And thank you for caring.

In his new book of poems, *To Be Now*, Marty Gervais
makes an art out of caring. He reveals again and again

how by paying attention, how by being fully alive and completely engaged, an artist might capture and transform into poems a profound understanding of lives. What Marty in mischief calls *lying*, is in fact a form of drawing from the deeper wells of truth that do not adhere slavishly to the facts, but rather arise from the clear depths of the soul where the inner truth resides. Whether he's writing about the bachelor farmer willing his body to science, or about the monk who sleeps all year under the stars, he reveals himself through his poems as a poet of the first rank. He sees in the trivial events and the smallest lives the possibility of largest meaning. Whether he's driving to Dresden through the winter night, or simply lying in the half-dark watching his wife undress, he gives us the gift of his words a glimpse into what it means to be human. Be here. Laugh. Cry. Think. Feel. Be grateful for these poems. They make a difference.

this poetry is for Donna

# One

# God's Lies

# New poems

# Leaving Your Body
# To Science

It is there in those hours
of a cluttered darkness
of this gabled farmhouse
in sheep country
that he thinks about
this, the mounds of
dust-covered magazines
and seed catalogues
and books and pill
bottles and tractor
parts spilling out over
the floor and around
the four-poster bed,
memories of a life
of rising before
dawn, and pulling on
coveralls and sipping
a cup of hot tea before
venturing out into
the cool fall air of
the late harvest fields,
this bachelor uncle with a
strong heart believing
he might have
something to offer
and tells everybody
when the time comes
— if it comes —

he'll leave this body
to science but no one
knows what arrangements
he's made, what calls
he might've made,
what inquiries,
and someone suggests
they ought to ask him,
ask him, meaning
what will happen
when he dies, where
will he be buried,
what does he want
said, and what about
this, this idea he has
of leaving his body
to science, and someone
asks, "Well, how do
you do that? I mean, how
do you go about leaving
your body to science?"
To this, the old bachelor
bristles, "You just
call them ... you just
call them and say, 'Come
get me!'" But his nephew
persists, "Call who?"
"Science!" barks
the bachelor uncle.

"Science?" repeats
the nephew, "D'ya
mean like 'Hello! This is
Science calling. Just
wondering when we can
get at that old body of
yours ...'" The old man
shrugs and wends
his way through the
florid wallpapered
hallway to his room
back to the clutter
to the refuge of darkness
and you can hear him
clearly far beyond
the creaky wooden stairs
"I'm not going to die."

# The Cow on the Bardstown Road

A man rides a truck
ahead of me from Bardstown
a cow in the back
shifting back and forth
with each new curve
of the road
its unsteady cow legs
doing a moon walk
on this clear afternoon
in March
I think of its sad cow eyes
drinking in the coming
of spring, of lush pastures
of blue skies
cumulus clouds
the warmth of earth
I think of its sad cow mind
speculating about change
and maybe about
the men and women
in the cars queuing up
behind this truck
and maybe about the
physics of speed
and sound and wind
along this road
I think of its sad cow eyes
dreaming of the earth

rushing by without her
A man rides a truck
ahead of me from Bardstown
adjusting the radio
heedless of the traffic
dreaming among the curves
of this road, eager
to bring home his new cow
eager to embrace
the security of spring

# Going Home

The mist over the monastery
its white walls faded
into the haze
the sun just peeking
over the stiff steeple
see the cemetery
I wade into the damp grass
My feet wet and
cold, think of a summer
morning as a youth
when I crossed a field
with a friend
a night of carousing
our eyes burning with
the new day, our
mouths tired from
so much laughing
our pant legs
soaked from the tall
weeds as we made
our way to a highway
always heading home
And today I stand on this
hill, see the outline of
the church emerging
like the face of a
saint forming in
the hands of a god
I see myself, a face

full of hope, believing in
the future, believing
in joy — yet
suspicious
forever confused
forever going
home

# God's Lies

I lie to you
try to trick you
promise things
that can't possibly
be done
After a while
I believe the lies
myself, and
wonder if you
took them all in
to wait the results
Wonder if you
were fooled, if
you had
the human capacity
to see through things
if you had the
naivete to
believe in the
impossible

I know you
can disappoint
— especially when
*you* can't deliver
but why do we
expect it? You never
promised results

All you
said was
you'd be there
to sit by us
to let the fear
work its way
through our blood
that worry
was no use
that hope
was eternal
was the only
ingredient the
soul needed
How can we
believe you? How can
we trust you? What's
the point of it all?
I guess the point is
to let go, open up
be ready, fearless
anxious, silent

# Prayers at the Hermitage

I step
out on the porch
at dawn
only my
underwear
a pair of slippers
letting loose the nightmares
that kept me close
to you —
I feel mad,
a lunatic rejoicing
at the sky taking shape
Like watching a film slowly
coming alive on the screen
and I sing to the clouds
to the monk's water
tower, the hills
the blueness
and wonder aloud
if this is what you
might have felt
that first day
of creation

# Pictures in the Shrine
## at Chamayo

I can smell the flowers
when I step into this
mission church...
See a woman kneeling
at the communion rail
She has just tucked
a photograph of her brother
into the corner of a
framed holy picture
a brother who died
of cancer two weeks ago
a brother who had
helped her across the
border from Mexico
four years ago, drove
her in a 1972 Ford pickup
at night, helped settle
her into a small house
here, helped her
find a job cleaning
the church, doing
laundry for the priest
cooking ... Now she
prays for her brother's soul
her hands wrapped
in beads, lips
trembling, and there's
her brother's picture
high up above

a tiny side altar
tucked in with a
picture of a saint
a smiling man of 45
from a time when
he knew nothing of
death, sickness
tragedy ... He knew
life, and took the risk
to bring his sister
and her children here
drove them 378 miles
mostly at night on
empty Mexican
highways ... His sister
sitting up front with
him in the cab with
an infant wriggling
the other kids cocooned
in blankets in the back
of the truck, fallen asleep
under the moon-filled
night ... She thinks about
that now and sobs, knowing
the risks he took, knowing
she could never repay
him except for this
— to pray for him
to place his picture there
among the saints ...

# The Glasses

Last night I dreamed
I put on my glasses
and walked through
the darkest parts of
my soul
where excuses
were just that, where
joy was beside the point,
where love was a far
fetched notion
With these glasses
I could see clearly
in the dark, peer at
the underside of
lies, all the
hopes, bravado,
the stuff that keeps
you living
keeps you
just this
side of death

# Hips

Like the curve
of a hockey stick
the soft bend in the road
at dusk, the way
a branch bows
with the full weight
of apples in the fall
I saw curves
everywhere —
I thought of all
the young girls whose
figures would blossom
with my adolescent
fantasies, their hips
swaying in the cool spring
the slope of the jeans
or the gingham dress
the way they moved
with unctuous grace
When I was 12
the deciding factor
my buddy told me
was a good set of hips
— the pick of a good
wife lay with the hips
perfect for childbearing
and we'd stand
on the street
at the Parkview Diner

and take inventory
of the young moms
size up their hips
cock our head
to one side
and nod in agreement
over the perfect set —
one as slender and lithe
as a  balsam tree, others
as wide and proud
as the bumper
of a Chev Impala
I had become
sexually aware at 12
silently measuring
the half-moon like
curves as they sauntered
down aisles, as they moved
between tables in the
school cafeteria
I saw curves
everywhere —
catching the Yankee
Billy Martin sliding
to one side to make
a play at second
his hips in the October
series like the elegance
of a cougar moving

to snare his prey
I saw hospital
pinstripers pouring
out at the end of a day
their lovely bodies
as smooth as a warm
current in the lake
I saw Elvis bump
and grind, his white
suedes flashing on
a darkly-lit stage
hips swiveling
like a well-oiled
engine
I saw curves
everywhere —
I didn't see breasts
I didn't fixate
on crotches
or the slope of
a neckline
or the nakedness
of thighs
I saw hips
I saw hips
I saw hips

# Knowing the Dancer
# from the Dance

The Cuban boxers loll
about the fenced yard
— tall and wearing
jackets in the heat
the faint breeze
of the Pacific wafting in
They laugh at a young
man in a nearby café
who is putting the make
on a dark-haired woman
twice his age
and they call to her
and point to themselves
and laugh again
at the frustrated man
who finally tosses
a bouquet of roses into the street
and walks off
With that one of the boxers —
urged on by the others —
gallops across the street
scoops  up the flowers
and offers them to the
woman who sits for a moment
— only for a moment —
then smiles, cocks her head
in a petulant way, pauses
then slowly wraps her arms

around the boxer's neck
and kisses him full on the lips
holding it a moment
— only a moment —
then gently all in one
motion, pulls away,
rises from her chair,
reaches for the small cloth
handbag at the edge of the
table, and turns and walks
away — the Cuban left
as stunned and bewildered
as if he had been caught by a left hook
he never saw coming

# Summer Earth
# Down the Road

*For John B. Lee*

Somewhere below the
summer earth in the field
down the road
the cemetery gates
bloom with roses
and you walk with the
family, there to bury
an aunt, to talk
about life, to inveigh
words softly
in the hot sun
of a morning after
the church service
words of consolation
and memory
of covenants made,
and contritions never
attempted —
And though no one
speaks about her
somewhere below the
summer earth in the field
down the road
is your baby sister who died
in your mother's arms
barely a day old
and though no one
has marked her grave

where now her small
bones lay in the
warm summer earth
next to your aunt
you think of that
little girl and
what she might've
become here and
now as you walk —
the tie so unnatural
in its knot for this
solemn occasion
the glare from parked
cars like the shine
on the stiff brogues
you wear for this day
You think of her
this sister who might've
said things better,
might've grappled
your father's arm
to tell him things
about his aunt
that a brother
might never understand

# This is What I Know about Penises

*For J.B.L.*

I have always had a little
trouble making it *plural*,
The word doesn't look right
when you add "es"
Doesn't sound right
to have more than one
at any one time
though there was a doctor
in 1609 in Wecker
who found a corpse
in Bologna with two penises
I lie in the bathtub
and think about what
you told me today
how you decided
to write an ode to your penis
as if it was your best friend
and wonder if Keats or
Shelly might've pondered
the same. Or how you
carry it with you
like a badge from
a secret society
how it never lets you down
But have you forgotten
those childhood years
when you wet the bed
at a sleepover at a friend's?

Or those times
in the schoolyard
when you weren't looking,
and someone tossed a football
and you bent over double
as the pain shot through you
like an electric charge
Or those moments
after so much adolescent
fumbling in the back seat
of a car, you lay back
sweating and humiliated
because at long last
you couldn't get it up
you couldn't make it work
Or those porno films
that made you believe
you were the only one
in the world that small —
I lie in the bathtub
and stare at my own —
it bobs in the soapy water
like an arrogant swimmer
and think of all the
names given it
over the centuries —
knob, dick, shumck, rod
tool, percy, John Thomas,

the bald headed mouse, the
yoghurt-spitting sausage,
Kojack's Moneybox,
the salty salami, Sergeant
with one blue stripe
who loves to stand
at attention, Captain Winky
the pink lighthouse that wants
to draw you onto its rocks
the sentimental teaser, the arrow
of desire, the crimson butterfly
the flute of love and
the blood-gorged meat club
I lie in the bathtub and
stare at it, as if it was
a neighbour's dog
that wouldn't stop barking
as if it was a car that suddenly
spun out of control
and struck a telephone pole
as if it was a new face at
school, someone else
to ridicule and mock
I think of penis sizes
the average being 3.5 inches
the longest 13 inches
how a man will average
11 erections in a day

and 9 at night, and
how in a life time
he will ejaculate 7,200 times
I think of the ancient Greeks
who worshipped it,
and paraded the streets
of Athens with six-foot phalluses
how the early Christians
saw it as the Devil's Rod
a thing of evil shape
how every March 15
the Japanese in the
small town of Komaki
throw a giant
festival to celebrate the penis
and parade the streets
with a 900-pound
phallus, and how women
carry massive dildos
in their arms
how the Caramjoa tribe
of Northern Uganda
tie a weight on the end
of their penises
to elongate it
how the men of the Walibri
tribe of central Australia
greet each other

by shaking penises
instead of hands
I think of the questions
surrounding it —
Is size important?
If not, why are
there no two-inch
pencil-thin vibrators?
Why would men rather lose
a leg than the family
jewels? Is masturbation
exciting because it is sex
with someone you pity?
And just who is the
captain of the ship?
Tell me ...
I lie in the bathtub
and wonder if it
could ever really be someone
else's best new friend ...

# On The Mirror

On the mirror in a room
in the house in which
my wife grew up
and where I retreat
on chaotic afternoons
I look at your
picture put there
so many years
ago — two of
us standing along
the canals in
Venice, a cold
afternoon in the spring
our bellies warm
from brandy
in a tiny bar
and we're about
to race to the train
back to Bologna
and we asked
this boy to take
our picture, like
Honeymooners
that dark afternoon
so long ago, so
far away from
our spouses
a day spent like
there was no tomorrow

and the talk till we
fell asleep on the
train just before
arriving in Bologna
That night, the constant
banging of shutters
and a sharp wind
whipping along
the narrow fish market
streets, the room
frigid, my head
swimming with
dreams, awaiting
the market men and
women to arrive
at 5 a.m.—
their songs in the darkness
and hearing them talk
as they sip hot coffee
below my room
I think about you now
so long ago, and what
might've been, what
might've happened
I sat on the edge of
that bed in Bologna
saying nothing
saying nothing

# The Cow Girl Hall of Fame

The girl at the bar
with a tray of beer
resting on the flat of
a hand, the cowboy
hat cocked back
the wispy blonde
hair, the muscles of
her right arm flexed
with the weight of
ten beers
a smile as warm
as the New Mexico air
the dim lights of
the bar just managing
to catch in her
eyes that I imagine
to be blue ...
I see the way
men look at her
the slight curves of
her body in the
deep pockets of
tavern darkness
as her body glides
lithely through a maze
of tables of men
and women laughing
the card players
not paying attention

at all except for
one man glancing
up from a set of
bad cards ...
She moves with
grace in a world of
chaos like a notion
an idea, like a moment
lost in pleasure
so fleeting...
I imagine her
going home after midnight
sighing at the door
taking a moment to
swing the cowboy hat
over a peg just inside
happy for her tiny
children in bed
and her man
sprawled, asleep on
the couch, the television
going and dishes piled
in the kitchen sink ...

# Before Sleep Takes Over

There are moments when
I see you  come into the
bedroom at night after
the lunches are made
the dog fed, the children
put to bed, the television
shut off, the heat turned
back, and I watch you
undress in the tungsten
light of the room,
the soft curve of a
shoulder, the outline
of your back, the same
woman I have known
for 32 years, and
I want to ask what you're
thinking, what you're feeling
right now, this moment
in this time, and I know
it's not enough to hold you
There are things you
want to say and won't
and you keep them, let
them sleep, let them stay
where they will in that
private place, and I wonder
just how much I know of
you, how much of you
is ready to give yourself

to the night, how much of
you is ready to let it go
And you turn to me
and smile, your eyes
sleepy, and somehow
that's enough, I guess,
somehow that's all that
you're ready to give
and I take it, and kiss
the warmest part of
your neck before letting
sleep take over

# He Couldn't Fix
# The Tractor

I take the highway
that runs past the tiny house
near the gas pumps
I mouth a silent prayer
for my mother who told us
about summer evenings
when her uncle the faith
healer stopped by, the
Studebaker turning into
the drive his neatly cut
pants the jacket, the lapel
bursting with a rose
his smile broad and the
hands, the slim delicate hands
of a man of prayer scrubbed
white and pink, the hands
that brought him money
and fame, the hands that
brought hope to
French families in the flat
lands of Essex County
My mother told me
he used to bound in through
the side door, bearing gifts
his eyes blue and penetrating
as they drank in the scene
in the big kitchen where
the men gathered at
noon, tired from chores

and her uncle would start
talking, the words that
would make the men forget
the fields, the work outside
forget the mortgage, the broken
down tractor and the hired
hand who waited by the
cement silo, waited for
the others to come
and my uncle would talk and
talk and talk, words of
hope, of God, and Christ
and Holy Ghost, of
Satan and Evil, of the broken
down tractor as a sign of
a contract broken with the
land with God and now it
was time to atone and the
men would listen to him
reaching as they did for
a pipe or chewing tobacco
as the afternoon turned
grey and cold, as his words
turned their thoughts
back upon themselves
and then he'd stride out
to the Studebaker parked
in the yard under the elms
and he'd still be talking
and that's when my mom

asked if he could fix the tractor
that stood still in the field
like a stubborn mule that
wouldn't move, and he knelt
down beside her — she, being
all of six years old — and he
said, "Honey I can fix bones
and muscles. I can fix fevers
and gout. I can fix bad eyes
and twisted limbs ... But
I don't know a damn thing
about tractors — that's for
someone else ... Man made
them!" And with that
her uncle swung open the
large shiny door of his
Studebaker, and wished
them well, said he'd pray
for the tractor ... That's about
all ... I think of him
and my mom that day
in the summer, maybe
it was 1924 ... Imagine
her standing on the bottom
step of that porch at the side
and her uncle's big car
sprawling in the summer sun
and the hands that couldn't
get the tractor started

# René

I heard terrible things
about him —
thief, deserter
communist
He had shown  up
at the farm
one afternoon
asking for a cup of water
My mémé handed him
a metal cup that
he took out to the pump
near the house
filled it two
or three times
cradling the sides,
precisely, methodically
drinking it down
like a boy trying not
to spill his milk
Filling it one more time,
gently directing
the cool well water
over his forearms
the back of this neck
— the heat and humidity
too much
That was the first time
they saw René —
he strode up the laneway

one afternoon
made his way back
down the dirt road
toward the lighthouse
Days later, back,
knocking at the side door
by the summer kitchen
Again, my grandmother
directed him to the pump
Kindly, polite —
he drank two
or three cupfuls
This time, my mémé
asked if he would stay
help out, and he agreed,
putting up
in an old chicken coop
near the barn
After a few weeks
he had made it into a home
tacked down a linoleum floor,
carried in an old cutting table
one chair, a propane
stove, a picture of
the Last Supper
torn from a book
At night you could
see him through the
lighted window

reading, sitting
in the only chair
leaning back on it
turning the pages
At dinner, my mémé
would send me
with a plate of dinner
hot turkey and potatoes
He'd open the wooden door
and the screen, just a
crack, the rough hands
reaching for the metal plate
and I remember peering up
wondering what
he was all about,
a thief that might raid
the house one night,
steal away with one of us
— his eyes as silent as
the open cornfields outside
the door, and finally, he'd
mutter something in French
and the door would shut
My brother Billy told me
he had been with the SS
in Germany, he was hiding
on the farm, that he
was Eichmen, maybe
Hitler's son — and one

day when he was out
in the fields, we invaded
the silence of his space
finding a breviary on
the gray blanket on
the cot, a stack of
papers from Paris,
a book by Proust
another by Cocteau
a war medal
and a flyswatter
hanging from a nail
on the door
We'd hoped for
pictures of Goebbles
or Rommel or Goering
or Hess — instead
we found
a solitary man
who clung to loneliness
like a jewel
Forty years later
— long after he had fled
the farm for the Canary
Islands — I still
searched the papers occasionally
anticipating his arrest
as a war criminal

# Running Into Daylight

It was the year the union
came into the plant, and
I heard my father talk
about it one night, and
watched him roll the
Toronto Star into a
tube as he spoke —
angry and worried
over the men organizing
at the head light factory
he managed, the paper
now like a torpedo in
his hand, and it was
strange the way he
kept rolling it, the
whole time talking
to my mom about a
possible strike, and
we knew there was
no point asking him
about buying
us a football, no point
asking him for the
money, no point
talking to him at all
He just kept talking
about the same thing —
things I had never heard of
before, unions, and strikes

and wages, and benefits
all the things I knew
nothing about at 12
but I listened from the
other room, hoping to
ask him about the football
about buying the one
downtown, so I could
play with my new friends
from the school
We had just moved
to this northern town
and I saw the football
as a way of buying my
way into the clique
I saw the football
as a way of winning
approval, knowing I could
throw it straight as
a missile, knowing
I could run it down
the field faster and
better than anybody
knowing it would
make the boys at school
talk about me, knowing
it would wipe away
that uncertain suspicion
about me as the new

boy in town
Besides, I had promised
them I'd come back
with the new ball
that my father would buy
it for me, that it would
be the game ball we'd
use against Gravenhurst
in the annual fall match up
But my father kept
talking about the union
all through dinner, and
long into the night
and I never got to ask
him if I could have
the money for the
ball, never got to tell him
what it would mean to
be a hero, what it would
mean to win, what it
would mean to run
into daylight, the boy
with legs like lightning

# Tell Me About Your Tomato Plants When I Can't Sleep

We might call it love —
this business of
telling each other
what really matters
what bothers us
on the worst days
what rankles us
and not so much
the petty things like
leaving off the top of
the toothpaste
or leaving behind
orange peels and
apple cores in the
car, those things that
make us fume and
swear under our breath
At night when
it's time to sleep
and you curl up
I find that I cannot sleep
that I've carried the
day with me into
this bed and lie there
wide awake
That's when I need you
That's when I implore you
to tell me about your
tomato plants —

I yearn to drift
to think of nothing
more significant than
this, the puny tomato
plants that sprout in
our garden, that fruit
September brings
the most boring of
all fruits ...
I then feel myself drift
drift in the soggy whisperings
you make of that
summer garden

# Shipping Out

They'd been out
drinking the night
before, dancing
at the grand dance
halls in Detroit
and they cursed
the old man
for catching them
asleep on their
watch and for making
them run for an hour
on the upper deck
rifles held high
over their
heads and they
cursed the sun
the smog and
cursed their lives
and the war that
yanked them out
of the factory jobs
and the old roadhouses
along the river
It was after that
they became buddies
and drank rum
And when they
shipped out across

the Atlantic on the
corvettes there
were nights
when they'd get
into the rum
to keep the hours
going, to keep
their nerves
in check, and it
was never easy
the yawing and
dipping of the ship
as it cut through
the Atlantic leading
the big carriers
across to Europe
watchful of the
German subs
And Tommie
would hang his head
over the side
letting his dinner
fly into the dark
night of the Atlantic
In those moments alone
in the mick
they'd chat, play
some poker, promise

the world to each
other, and when
they were in port
Tommie would
always come to
Casey's rescue, snatching
him from barroom
fights, drumming
some other sailor
over the head
with a chair
And one night
he stopped his
buddy from tossing
a slot machine into
the harbour
It was on the
Shawinigan that night
Casey told Tommie
that when he got
married he'd be his
best man
Tommie said "You'd
better consider that
because I *am* you're
best man ... Nobody
else can take my place!"
When the war was over

and Tommie had gone
back to his wife
and the job at Ford's
he was sitting
on the porch one afternoon
when Casey drove up
And Casey told him,
"I'm sorry I've got bad news
for you — my family's
pressuring me to
have my stepbrother
be the best man."
Tommie stood up
and for a moment said
nothing at all — his
ruddy face rigid and
angry, his eyes flashing
like a summer storm
"After all we've been
through, and you'll still
do that, then there's
nuthin' between us!"
For the next 20 years
Tommie wouldn't talk
to Casey, never called him,
never gave him a thought
Until one afternoon
Casey stopped by where

Tommie had been working
and the two stood
at the plant entrance
In that instant
the years evaporated
and Casey told Tommie
how sorry he was
how the marriage
never worked out
how so many times
he had wakened in
the night, and started in
with the rum, and would
run from one room to
the other, slamming
doors, and then push
past the screen door
to the porch and go
out to the yard,
and stand there
looking up at the night
sky and scream
how sorry he was,
how he had been
wrong, so wrong ...

# The Farmers' Chapel

The pickups parked in
chaotic zigzags in the
darkness, men and
women from nearby
farms here for mass
in the monastery chapel
one man at the back
nervous as he jingles
coins in his pocket
a woman fidgeting
with an umbrella
trying to smooth out
its damp contours
like my grandmother
who used to run her
hand over the table
cloth, feeble hands
flattening out the
creases, a man clearing
his throat and someone
else turning about
in his direction, and
the man stops for
now anyway, a woman
staring at her shoes
and finally reaching
down with a piece of
tissue to wipe away
some soil from the toe
Mass at 6 a.m.

I had raced down
to the farmers' chapel
watching the lightning
break over the rounded
hills, hearing distant
thunder and noticing
the farmers' pickups
turning into the laneway
the lights rigid and
swinging out over
the tall grass — and
my sudden shadow
looming large because
of it, and there I am —
I thought — like
a boy again on the way
to the winter chapel
of my youth to serve
mass for the old
Irish monsignor
There I am again —
this time cursing the
morning darkness, or
the wine — too much
of it from the night
before — There I am
again at the boarding
school in Northern Ontario
hastening to the mass

— flattening out my hair
doing up the buttons of
my uniform — always
rushing some place
But there I am —
the farmers and their
wives in the chapel
their caps on the seats
behind them as they stand
and praise this new day
their thoughts like mine
on other things, things
maybe not God's and
things maybe not sacred
But what does it
matter? We quiet our souls
we shut down the engines
we sit, we clasp our
hands — we hear our
hearts beating maybe
for the first time in years
like a boy standing
in a parking lot and
suddenly looking up
at the night sky
standing there in wonder
at the speckled-lit sea
of night

# The Hockey Equipment

I sat near the back step
of the apartment just
above the bank
and tried on the equipment
— shin pads, shoulder pads,
elbow pads, helmet
The bank manager's wife
stood there watching me,
said I could have them
they had been her son's
she would just throw them
out if I didn't take them
I lugged the bag
home that night up main
street to my house,
and dumped it out
on the basement floor
and tried it all on
again in silence, but for
the hum of the coal furnace
That winter I played
my heart out trying to
make the travel team
and didn't and wound
up playing early Saturday
mornings with boys as
bad at hockey as I was
I remember noticing the
bank manager's wife

coming out a few
mornings to watch
She just sat at one end
of the arena under the
advertisement for the
dry goods store, same
spot a couple or three
Saturdays in a row
then I didn't see her again
All winter I wondered
about why she had come
and wondered about her boy
and what happened to him
whether he ever made
the hockey team
I couldn't remember
his name, though she must've
told me, couldn't think of
what it was, and where
was he anyway? I was
new to town and didn't
know the stories, the
families, except for my
my new friends, and
maybe I scored a half
dozen goals, and by
the end of March
I was packing away the

equipment in the basement
and thought of her son
again and finally asked
a buddy of mine —
who the bank manager's son
was and he told me
two winters before I moved
to town their son had fallen
through the ice on
the south branch
of the river, playing
hockey, had been on the
travel team, a goal
scorer, hands like Jean
Beliveau, and he was 15
and the *Bears* were looking
to sign him next season
The next winter when
I opened the bag —
the embarrassment was
overwhelming, of how
badly I had played the winter
before, how the boy's
mother sat there those
Saturday mornings
in hope of catching
the grace and glory of
a son she no longer had

# The Men Outside
# Mary's Bar

The men were drinking
on the porch outside
Mary's Bar, saluting the
hot afternoon air with
their beer cans
They spotted the
women in the car
especially the blonde
who stepped out with
her camera to take
their picture
and the one man
with the leather coat open
exposing a bare chest
stepped forward into
the empty main street
and said, "Where you
all from? You
want my picture!"
The other women
stepped out of the car
and started circling around
to join their friend
and this fellow turned
to his buddies on the
porch and muttered something
then turned around
"No problem — want

our picture, all of us?"
And the blonde woman
said, "Hey, that would be
great! (pause) And we're
from Texas!" And raised her
camera to her eyes
when the man pumped
his arm in a count of
three and the three men
pulled down their
pants one by one
and mooned the women
— three bare bums in the
afternoon street of this
tiny town in the south
as if they had choreographed
this moment for days
just for the amusement
of themselves or these
women, and the blonde
put down her camera
turned to look at her friends
then back again at the men
and said, "Just hold
it there boys!"

# The Phone Call

I saw the man on the phone
and wondered why he
was making that call
maybe to a girlfriend
maybe he was cheating
on his wife and had to
go down to the only phone
booth at the edge of town
the middle of the afternoon
when his wife
was cleaning out the back
room for her mother's
visit later this month when
the woman at Mary's Bar
was sitting on the sofa
by the window lost in
an old dime store novel
when all the dogs were asleep
when there was nothing to
do but talk ... I imagine
this man promising his girlfriend
how he was going to get
away, and I watch him
and see his truck baking in
the hot afternoon sun
I see him shift back
and forth, the cowboy
boots kicking up the sand

below the booth, and see
the hat cocked back as he
smooth-talked this lover
saying he can't make it tonight
and how much he'd love
to slip in beside her that night
when she's off work
from the co-op, and
how he's thinking how good
it feels each time he climbs
into his truck a little after
midnight to make his way
back  home — the cool night
on his arms as he rides with
the windows down, the
excitement of having just
left a beautiful young woman
in his life, a woman much
younger than him, and
the idea of lying to his wife
and how she believes
everything he tells her —
how he had been working
late and couldn't get back
home, how he had thought of her
and wanted to call but couldn't ...
Deep down this cowboy
knows the way he feels about

his wife, how she'll be up the
next morning with poached
eggs on the plate, hot coffee
on the stove, a tender hand
on the back of his neck
as he sits at the table
He knows nothing will change
her notion about him ...
That's why he's there
on the phone ...

# The Room At The Top of the Stairs

I sit in the upstairs room
The window glittering
with ice from last night's
storm, the room we used
to sleep in when we
came to visit your
parents, those hot summer
evenings, the factory
sounds nearby and trains
shunting at the end
of the street in the
dead of night, and
how I couldn't sleep
and would turn
in the bed, the moonlight
across your face and arms
and I'd wonder then
what would become of us
where we might end up
Tonight I think
of what we went
through, those moments
when lies helped
us through days
when loneliness
caused us to make
mistakes — or at least
that's what you told me

I find it hard to forgive
as did you back then
I find it hard to stop
thinking about what
went wrong, what
consumed us for so
many years, why we
danced apart, our glances
moving into things
that really didn't matter
or seemed to then
Tonight I dream of you
the way we were in those
pure moments, the park
shimmering in snow
that first Christmas together
the soft fall of pine
needles to the hardwood
floor in the other room
as we learned to
be with one another
for the first time
our bodies new and
fresh our minds full
of innocence our mouths
telling truths

# The Woman on the Beach at Hanlan's Point

There were moments when
things had gone awry
but hearing your voice
over the phone after maybe
20 years, I see you on
the beach at Hanlan's Point
an army jacket wrapped
around your young
body, and I roll
awake on the hard
sand, my arms and
chest heavy with
the night before
sleeping on the
windy island
I see the sun rising
over the lake so full
and fat it looks too heavy
and tired to haul itself
back up and I notice
the fire is low, and
see you rising to
gather up broken
branches and beach
debris to feed the flames
and I'm thinking of
coffee, of the Café May
on Roncesvalles

but we're here on
the beach, a Monday
morning in the summer
with nothing else to
do but patrol the
empty sand at this
early hour, and
I remember your
eyes, the freckles
your hair long and
blonde the long legs
the small hands
and the smile
Seems all so romantic
and it was.
By the summer of '68
I was hitching rides
out west, crossing the
prairies, sleeping in
cheap motels, finding
my way down to
this city on the border
finding a room by
the week, a flop house
above a bar, the
drunks and prostitutes
and I'd sit there
and write about you

about what might've
been, what might've
happened, and now
after all these years
your voice awakens
in me something
I can't comprehend

# To Be Now

He slipped his arms
around her waist
and took a stroll
along Woodward Ave.
past the vaudeville
theatres, the old boxing
clubs, the men and
women lolling about
in the cold
and she could feel
the wind whipping up
and around her legs
and she hooked
one arm around
his and held him close
and bent her head slightly
toward the chilly gusts
coming off the river
and he asked if
she wanted
to see the Red Wings
and she shrugged
Nothing else mattered
right now
except to be here
to be with him
to be here
to be now

And so they walked
to the Olympia
and she never complained —
her new high-heels
clicking on the pavement
and he talked about
the season the Wings
were having, those
big farm boys with
hands as large as snow shovels
and she pretended
to be interested
but really all she
thought about
were the high heels
she'd ordered out
of the catalogue
and the day
they arrived —
her hands trembling
with excitement
how she held the
shoes like delicate birds
in her hands
and how the winter sun
poured through
the parlour window
and she imagined

walking with him —
this tall sheep farmer
whose manner was
gentle, whose promises
were true, and now
there she was strolling
with him — their
honeymoon in Detroit
nothing else mattered
right now
except to be here
to be with him
to be here
to be now

# Under the Weight of Heaven

*For Paul Quenon*

You sleep in the tool shed
by the road under the stars
at the back of the monastery
and tell me about the lovers
— the farm boys
with their sweethearts
who steal into the night
when all is asleep here
and park their cars
in the holy stillness
and after a while
quietly drive back out
to the highway
You hear their cars
mounting the hill beyond
and hear them disappear into
the splendid darkness
You sleep in the tool shed
by the road under the stars
and awake suddenly to
an unfamiliar sound
on the road
and look up and see
the enormous shape
of a horse like a mountain
emerging from the mist
in the early morning

but only a horse
a mare that has strayed from
a nearby farm
It lolls about
under the swaying weight
of the heavens
You sleep in the tool shed
by the road
under the stars
and wake to the morning
with the bells beckoning you
to vigils — then you see
this work horse lying
in the dark meadow
and nod to her as you would
a friend, and say good morning
then make your way to chapel
You sleep in the tool shed
under the stars
where the world
comes to you
— silent guests who steal away
your sleep, who leave you
wondering, who leave you
undisturbed, alone
You sleep in the tool shed
under the weight of Heaven ...

# That Summer Day
# You Came Home
*On Rosemary's 50th Birthday*

I saw you that morning
in the summer
the sky a slate colour
gray and our mother
stepping from the
Plymouth, her foot
resting a moment
on the gravel
driveway
as she braced
herself to lift you
I saw her smile
as she looked up
to the kitchen window
where I stood
my face pressed
to the glass to
see my only
little sister
I was four
and had to
stand on a chair
at the window
and for a moment
wondered why
all the fuss
as our mother
lifted you in her arms

the blanket slightly askew
as she carried you
from the car to
the back door
I heard the screen
door slapping behind
as she mounted
those three steps
to the kitchen
and for a moment
I was a little put out
because she
brushed past me
didn't even look
down at me there,
so tiny I was —
At eye level to you,
I spotted those
dark eyes of yours staring
at me, so confused
they were, and
I smiled at you
for the first time
believing you were
my newest new friend

# Driving to Dresden

*For Donna*

You sleep beside me
in the car as we make
our way through wintry
darkness to a Friday
night arena
to see our boy play hockey
We wind our way in
darkness, the fields
flat in the open, the
orange lights of barns
and houses spilling
onto the powdery
white lawns, the single
yard light near
the barn, and a
man walking
from a pickup
to a house,
and a woman
standing with the
door slighty ajar
calling him
and he's saying
nothing, just coming
toward the house
and their lives
lift in me, make
me wonder about us

the reasons we
say things that
hurt or say
things that
make us believe
in love again
You sleep now
as we make
our way silently
through the snowy
night to this arena
in the cold light of
a moon to watch
a son who might raise
his head a moment
before a face off
to see if we're there
in that Friday night
arena, to see if
we dream
as he does
for that perfect
moment when he
finally moves like the
promise of spring

*Two*

# The Science
# of Nothing

# Lost And Found

The winter I was 13
I started collecting gloves
It began with
a man's leather glove
from Sears found
in the snow
after I pushed someone
out of a driveway
and I yelled after him
and he stopped
and rolled
down an icy window
and I dangled this
glove disfigured by
tire tracks but
he waved it off
saying it wasn't his
I took it home
and threw it
in the corner
of the hallway
with winter boots
and coats and didn't
think anything of it
until the next day
when I spotted
a kid's cotton
mitten with white
reindeer stitched

across the top
and there was
no one around
at the school
where I found it
and I thought of
knocking on someone's
door but few kids
lived in that neighbourhood
Again I took it home
and threw it in the
corner promising
to bring it to school
the next day for
the lost and found
but forgot about it
It wasn't until
a few days later
I found a woman's
glove, a narrow
delicate size,
and imagined
elegant fingers, someone
who played Bach
It was then
I rummaged in
the corner to
retrieve the other
two gloves

and went down
to the basement
and tacked
the three to a wall
For a long time I stared
at them — characters
in a novel, the people
to whom they belonged
their histories
what separated them
in that split second,
that instant when this
possession was liberated
set free like a caged bird
and how they searched
in their coat pockets
and stood there in
the street
next to their car
fumbling for keys
and glanced about them
on the ground
how they finally
got into the car
and scanned the floor
even leaned over to look
under the seat
and down the seat
near the door

and finally gave up
and drove away — the
other glove, the twin
tucked alone in a pocket
And as they drove
they searched again
absently believing it
might still be there
like a mother running
her hand in a gentle
circular motion over
the slight swell of her
belly in pregnancy
believing in life in
the future in all
things good and true
and there I was
standing in the dimly
lit basement of my
childhood home
staring at three gloves
By the end of that winter
I had 16 gloves —
7 men's, 4 women's
and five kid's —
tacked up on my wall
and the only name
— the only real name —
was that of Emily

a deer skin mitten
I fancied as belonging
to a 16 year old girl
The name, marked
inside in straight up
and down letters
perfectly and patiently
spaced, but there was
no one in town with
that name —
a town of 2,900 people
No Emilys, not
even Emilena,
I preferred it
that way
Years later a month
after my father died
as I shifted
boxes to a truck
outside, boxes from
his house
I flipped open
the lid to find
15 gloves and mittens
bound together by
an elastic band
and noticed the one
with Emily's name
had gone missing

# The Politician's Wife
*For S.C*


They had gone back
to the Legion
after the funeral
of the MP's wife
and the Irish band
had struck up
foot-stomping tunes
and her friend
—at her side
when she died —
paused a moment
in a long dark coat
draped over her shoulders
started to dance
— tentative, whimsical
Few noticed her
— perched awkwardly
as they were
on straight wooden chairs,
balancing Styrofoam cups and
paper plates of cold cuts
salads, meat balls
speaking of the loved one
All the while
her friend whirled,
her ankle-length coat
now whipping the air
as she gained momentum

tears streaming
her body moving effortlessly
till suddenly something
flew from her coat pocket
skittering across the floor
slipping finally under
the lunch tables
And she stopped —
cupped her face in
horror, then slowly
moved to pick up
what had been flung
from her coat
— her dead friend's teeth
Her shock soon
turned to giggles
as she recalled
that fateful afternoon
only a few days before
at the post office
how the politician's wife
— in the middle of telling her
about her husband
returning from Ottawa
for Christmas —
had toppled backwards
like a forlorn garden statue
smashing her head

on the marble floor,
falling unconscious
suffering a stroke,
She knelt down beside
her — wanting
desperately to help —
and removed the dentures
from the silent gaping mouth
of the MP's wife
then absent-mindedly
shoved them into
her coat pocket
The politician's wife
was already dead ...
Afterwards the family
couldn't find the dentures
couldn't believe
she would've gone
downtown without them,
and searched the lobby
but nobody asked her friend
and her friend
didn't know
the poor woman had
gone to her grave
without her teeth
Now there her friend was —
wearing the coat

for the first time
since that afternoon
and there in the pocket
were those remarkably
white teeth lying
in the naked palm
of her hand and
slowly she began
to dance again
and everyone looked
up from their coffee
to watch her throw back
her head, to let her
hair fly in abandon
and laughing
now laughing
and laughing

# Stopping By The House

We head along the road
by the church to the falls
this first day of the New Year
Stop by Joe's house
and stand inside by the
back door waiting for him
to come downstairs
his father pouring himself
a cup of coffee, fiddling
with the radio, not
saying a word as we peer
into the kitchen with
the big gas stove
A year ago almost
to the day
his mother died
in a hospital bed
wheeled into that kitchen
He had wanted her home
to take care of her
to be by her side
They tell us when she died
she complained about
the dishes in the sink
how he turned away
to wash two cups, a plate
some silverware
there in the dull light

of that room, quiet only
for the clatter of dishes
the hiss of the gas stove
and she died
He had turned to say
something but she was gone
and he stood there
leaning like he was now
against the cupboard
waiting for Joe
to return from choir practice
And when Joe did
Joe  knew something
was wrong, just in the way
his father looked at him
That was a year ago
and Joe isn't thinking about it
or so we think as he pulls
on his coat, pauses at the door
picks up a paper bag
says something to his father
And we're off running
along the river road
to Willy's Park
and Joe gallops ahead
his voice muffled by the
wind and we see him turn
into a laneway leading to

the cemetery, and
open the iron gate
We follow him as he makes
a pathway through the snow
across a hill of headstones
and there on a spot where
you can see the river
dazzling in the cold sunlight
Joe kneels and gently removes
a bright red poinsettia
from the bag
and places it
at the site of his mom's grave
After a moment
he looks up, his face
suddenly as bright as a new toy
and calls to us that he'll beat
us to the river
Off he runs, sliding among
the grave stones as he
races for the fence
and in that instant
he disappears over the hill ...
Today I remember him
my buddy from the drug
store, his father a painter
using the wooden backs of cigar
boxes to sketch lakes

and the late spring sugaring
and my buddy accompanying him
how he'd sit and paint with his
father, how they'd never
talk about her ...
It was years later
I came across him at
Alongquin and we talked
about that New Year's Day
1961, how it was the last
time he had left flowers
at his mom's grave, how
he never went back
anymore, how he felt
the distance his father
had known, and how his
father, only a week after
her death, had gone out
to the woods, and sat
there, a box of paints
on his lap, his fingers frozen
but painting the river
and the way the mist
rose like her spirit
in the soft cold light of
that January morning

# Picture Taking
# After The War

The film sputters and jerks
as the image suddenly
fills the screen and there
pouring out of the church
is an explosion of white —
white crinoline and starched
white shirts and bow ties
and praying hands
tucked in at the chest
and pointed upwards
to the Almighty
and Sister Mary running
up and down the
aisles poking everybody back
in line as the priest reviewed
the First Communion Class
like Eisenhower, his bald head
glistening in the spring sunlight
I see my sister
moving into place
and squinting at the sun
behind me and pictures
being snapped and my
father's friend operating
this 1950s movie camera
Finally, we pile into
the Plymouth and head home
There in the backyard

among rhubarb and tulips
and lilac trees
we gather for pictures
It's like that on Sundays
and I watch my father
sliding over to one side
to stand next to me,
then taking my sister's hand
and I'm looking down
at that coupling
wondering whose hand I'll take
I look from left to right
then down again at their
clasped hands
Suddenly I'm shoved aside
to let my grandfather in
beside my father
That look of bewilderment
lasts only an moment
as suddenly my father's hand
is in the picture again
jutting out from
one side of the frame
I see nothing else but it
grabbing me by the collar
of my white shirt
yanking me back into place,
I pull back, my face

like a gargoyle's grimace
and wonder about
those Sundays and
the people in that picture
my grandfather with his
silly Sunday pants yanked
up and belted almost to his chest
my father with the Clark Gable
mustache, dead, my mother
pregnant with another sister,
dead, and a neighbourhood boy
— not really a friend —
whose face popped from behind
the corner of the house
just for an instant and
how he pulled back to
stay out of sight
to stay out of the picture
 — now dead, drowned one
summer years later at Point Pelee
Only my brothers are
alive, and my sisters
We never see each other
never telephone never
write never keep up
Now there I am —
a Sunday night in the
basement playing back

this old film, marveling at
its grainy pockets, how
those figures leap off the screen
at me like ghosts of when
things were never perfect
I find myself swallowed up
by its confusion as if
someone is about to reach out
and snap me back into line
back into line

# Dragging Buses
# With Your Teeth

*For Stéphane*

The only thing
I was good at
was table hockey
and there was a time
when I'd retreat to
the backroom of the
newspaper bureau
and play the guys
in circulation
and make them buy me lunch
but I was terrible
on the ice, couldn't
stand up on my skates
couldn't score a goal
even if there was
an open net and pylons
directing the way to the net
I'd screw it up somehow
and last night
when I got off the phone
with a scout from Montana
who's looking at signing
my second oldest son
I wondered about it all
For years I've been standing
behind the glass
at the boards
watching my boys cutting
across the ice

their eyes fixed
on the puck
their bodies as swift
and clean and graceful
as a hawk above
a morning meadow
I wonder about it
where they learned this
where they found
that inherent
skill that natural
beauty that way
about them as they
float before a goalie
with all the confidence
of a magician playing
out a slight of hand
It couldn't be me
There were no Gervais
of any great hockey
talent, hell, sports
ability — except one
a guy from Montreal
who in the '50s could
pull buses with his teeth
if you call that sports
He'd strut out on
St. Catherine Street
clad only in a bathing suit

and he'd strap a rope
or wire of some kind
to the front of the bus
and use a special mouth
piece and slowly
with businessmen, housewives
and kids crowding him
would gently move
this lumbering old bus
along the street
That's it —
the rest of us
all failures when it
comes to pucks or baseballs
or tennis rackets or
swimming or anything
We were good with
words —grandsons of
a liar, sons of an
inventor and we wound up
selling shoes, insurance
became writers or priests
or telephone solicitors
made our living
with words, trotting out
Truth and Glory and Greatness
making people believe
the unbelievable

# The Queen's Annual Christmas Address to the Commonwealth

It was Christmas morning
when I went off down
the wintry street
down along the
storefronts, all shut
up, Christmas skates
slung over my shoulders
a brand new hockey stick
in my hands, and I made
my way to a friend's house
and he was waiting
for me with his new
skates and we trekked
over the ridge
from where you could
see the clock tower
of the old post office
It was now 10:30 a.m.
We skated that morning
on the Muskoka River
on the south branch
just back of the lumber yard
— the stillness in the sunlight
shattered by our voices
our skates cutting into the cold,
the slapping of sticks
and maybe the bells
of St. Joseph's Catholic Church

I remember that because
a neighbor had come
down around the river
and told my buddy he
was wanted at home
We sat on the river bank
to take off our skates
He needled me about the Leafs
blanking the Canadiens
in a game where it was clear
the Rocket had lost his
magic touch
We made our way back
to the house, still laughing
I followed him in
His mom was there to take
our wet coats and hang them
near the gas stove to dry
I noticed something was wrong,
her face was red from crying
I spotted the tissue wadded up
and tucked into the right sleeve
of her dress
She led my buddy to the parlour
and whispered to him
how her brother had died
how they had just gotten
a long distance call from London

that there had been some
kind of accident and he was dead
In the midst of all that
came the message
on the radio, blipping out across
the silent room
— the Queen's Annual
Christmas address to
the Commonwealth
We stood there in the parlour
— the faded wallpaper
of autumn leaves, the tin ceiling
I saw my buddy's mom sitting
still on the sofa, a tea cup
balanced on her lap, her face
turned to the window
And my buddy stared at
the floor — I had never
heard the Queen's voice before
never heard how she puckered
those vowels, rounded out
nouns and pointed her verbs
like torpedoes
I had never heard anyone
talk about peace, the yearnings
of those suffering
We stood still in a timeless pose
as if the monarch had known

all along about the news
having just befallen
this family
that morning

# My Son and
# Samuel Beckett

My son has put
a CCM hockey helmet over
a bust of Samuel Beckett
on top of the TV
and he watches
the Red Wings win
the cup and he tells me
every once in a while
he doesn't know who
this "Beckett" guy
is, and doesn't really
want to know — it's
better that way,
the lined face, the
quizzical eyes
He calls him the wise
old man of hockey,
a silent Don Cherry
and he thinks maybe
it brings good luck
to the games, his own,
for just as he runs out
the door with his
hockey bag, he reaches
for the helmet and kinda
looks at Beckett's face
and gives him the
thumbs up

# The Kid

*For W.O. Mitchell*

You entertained my kids
with magic tricks —
disappearing quarters
found behind  the ears
cards that floated in
the emptiness
above the dining room table
You would sit with my
seven year old son
and watch the games on
television, show him
how Lafleur could
cast a spell over the Forum
as he sped over the blue line
a slap shot like the finality
of heavy equipment crashing
to the floor
And a few years ago
you asked my boy
if he would go on television
with you for a Christmas
show where you would
read from a short story —
terribly shy, he ran off
to his room, eyes
full of tears
and you spoke to him
"What is it you want

the most this Christmas?"
"Bauer Supreme skates!"
he said after a moment
"You got it!"
And you went back
to the station and
told'em to write it
in the contract
And that Christmas
the skates were under
the tree
*from* W.O.
A month later,
You were  there in the
arena sitting
in the frozen seats
to watch my son —
cheering him, bellowing
out "Those are the skates
I got him!" as my boy
popped in five goals
and there you were
everybody knowing you
the shock of white hair,
voice booming in the arena
my son floating like
his hockey hero —
firing from an impossible

angle, the puck
sailing into the net
like a punchline
at the end of a poem
Twelve years later
I'm at your house
They've wheeled
in a hospital bed
into the kitchen
Now you lie as silent
as a stubborn dog
and no matter what I say
you say nothing
nothing at all —
until I mention
my boy, how he's
playing in Czechoslovakia
and your eyes brighten
a half smile —
And though you say nothing
I can hear the cheering
in a cold winter
across the ocean.

# The Galaxy

You could never get
a straight answer
out of Ron —
he'd tell you the car
would be ready tomorrow
and tomorrow would come
and he'd say he had
to order a part
and it would be ready
Friday, and Friday
would come and
he'd say the part
they sent was
the wrong one
It would now be Monday
or Tuesday before
he'd get the part
and maybe Wednesday
before he'd get'er done
After a while it seemed
Ron had the car more
than we did
Times when he'd surprise
us — getting up
on a frozen winter morning
there'd be our Austin Healey
sitting pretty under
the window, snow on

the hood, like a new bike
left in the middle of the night
by some good father
eager to please
his neglected children
That was Ron
Ron with a smile as
big as an Amway salesman
wrench in one hand
bottle of coke in the other
Times when I'd call
and his wife would answer
and turn away from the
phone and yell to him
that it was me on
the line and I could hear
cursing and the clangor
of tools and metal
being slammed down
Finally Ron would pick
up the phone friendly
and all, *How're ya doin'*
*Marty? So what's up?*
And I was always reticent
to incite him with a reply
like, *Dah! What's up?*
*You stupid ass. Where's*
*my car?* But I'd just ask,

*Well, just wonderin'*
*About my car?*
Why I kept going back
I don't know — he was
the only one who fixed
those English sports cars
Best in the business
But rarely did we ever
see the car — days would
stretch to weeks, to a month
One day I asked for a loaner
and without hesitation
Ron ambled out back
to get his own car
I could hear an engine
firing up, revving in short
blasts, followed suddenly
with billowing dust
from around the side
gravel flying against
the cement-block garage
The big Galaxy 500 approached
like the Marlboro man
and headlights as powerful
as howitzers
It made me wonder why
he gave me this —
the gas tank lay in the trunk

the lid flopped up
and down till we got some
binder twine and anchored
it to the chrome bumper
I wondered if I was
driving a Molotov cocktail
instead of a Ford
That was fine — it
was wheels
at least until that morning
when I sped along the highway
between Fergus and Guelph
and I went to pass someone
my foot to the gas pedal
the Galaxy V8 engine
practically leaping
like a pike wild on my line
when suddenly the gas pedal
and all the linkage crashed
through the floorboards
to the highway below
I had to steer this beast
to the edge, let it die
like an old work horse
in the silence
of that summer morning —
As for the Austin
I must've poured a couple

of thousand into it
till I owed so much
Ron had to sell it
I still wondered
if he'd ever really fixed it
I hadn't seen it for months
when he asked for the
ownership to be signed over
and we agreed
After a while I lost touch
with Ron — it was like
losing a brother though
once I got a postcard
that said he'd miscalculated
and I still owed
him $76.13
I never wrote back

# After The Fire
*For Donna*

Before I met you
maybe only a few weeks
that fall, nineteen sixty-eight
the man down the hall
retching, cursing the Tigers
though they'd win it all
in the end, cursing McLain
for throwing the game
That fall, I burned down
the hotel where
I'd been living
Not intentionally
I'd tossed the butt
of a cigarette down
an abandoned laundry chute
Stupid, never believing
what would happen
When I got down to
the paper where I
was the night reporter
it must've been 40 minutes
later I was rushing out
to cover the fire
boldly asking authorities
how it had started
knowing full well
I had ignited the blaze
It wasn't long after

we met
— I had moved from
the hotel where
you could hear
the hookers through
wallpaper-thin walls
and where I came to
believe the man next door
would soon put a fist
through the wall in
a drunken rage
if the Tigers didn't start winning
I got sick from coughing
from the wet charcoal stench
that hung in the air
after the fire
Had I not started the fire
I might have gone on
living there, and I might
not ever have met you
because later
after moving to a neat
and tidy room in a house
owned by an Italian
I stopped you on
the street, and brought you
back there, and over the next few
weeks we were married

and living somewhere else
I wouldn't change a thing
but I might lie about
the fire if someone
starts coming around
I'll tell them it's a metaphor
for something else
still burning inside

# The Hero

*For Robert Hilles*

I told my youngest kid
when I was a boy
these bullies started
picking on me
in the schoolyard
when suddenly
a large black hand
gripped the shoulder
of one of the bigger
kids and told him
"I wouldn't do that
... If you want a fight
you'll have to fight me"
And when the bullies
wheeled around to
see whose voice
this was
they were staring
at the bravado
of Mohammed Ali
and promptly ran off
"Is it true? Is it true?"
asked my son
I wanted him to
believe it was,
that Ali had come
to my rescue
It was like so many

other things —
I'd tell my other children
how I'd fought
at Normandy
how I'd been in hand
to hand combat
just outside
Hitler's bunker just
before he shot
himself
I told them I'd
played hockey
a few months with
the Rangers
but quit
to become a writer
Told my oldest son
I was good with my hands
but never had
time for carpentry
changing the oil
on my car or fixing
the toilet or putting
new washers
on the taps
I told him I could do
all this stuff but
if his mother knew

she'd be after me
to tackle all
these jobs
and how deliberate
I was in faking it
and just didn't have
the time
I told my children
things they wanted to hear
things they wanted me
to be, and never
figured they'd believe
any of it
They laugh about it now
laugh about
being taken in, duped
about standing
in silent admiration
I was none of these
I was born a year
after the Second
World War, I was
thrown off the
house league
hockey team
in Bracebridge
because I couldn't
stand up on skates

I failed "shop" at
high school
trying desperately
to make a plumb bob
and once cried
over my bicycle
at the end of
autumn on a frozen
street up north
because someone
had disassembled it
and I couldn't
get it back together
I was none of
the things I said
I was, and
I wonder if that's
why I changed
my name half
way through high
school
I remember you
telling me how
you'd told your
own children
everything in your childhood
had been black and white
meaning *television*

but Austin, your son,
started thinking
everything
in the world was
black and white,
trees and houses
and flowers
even the sky and
water, and in
a way he was
right — and you
were right — the
cars were black,
only black, and
floor tiles were black
and white and so
were  baseball
uniforms,
pictures in the papers
and wedding dresses
were white and
men's tuxedos black
even  politics
were black and white
You were right
in telling him that
And when I got
the chance to interview

Ali for the paper
years later, I shook
his hand, recalled
that story, the
smiling and defiant
face ordering those
schoolyard bullies
to scram
And when I went
home to tell my
son his eyes brightened
"So it is true?"

# II
# Scenes from the Present

# The Liar
# and the Inventor

My father was an inventor
my grandfather a liar
and it bothered my
father how his own father
would tell us stories
how he'd twist us
around a tale
— most of them untrue —
till we yearned
for the smallest details
and would settle
for nothing less
My father invented
other things, patented
energy-saving
devices, a type
of mayonnaise,
a bread knife
but he couldn't
spin a story
to save his soul
It seemed life
was lodged in his heart
like a stone
and he couldn't extract it
couldn't tell anyone
his fears, joys
or anything

Today I stare
in the mirror
see my father, cover my
lips, see his
nose, same eyes
the stern brow
I see all the things
I can't do, ordinary
simple things that
make sense, that
make life easier,
more efficient, safer
I see the words
that aren't his
but my grandfather's —
that loquacious style
a lot of nothing
a world of invented
images
adventures
lies

# At This Late Hour

We lounge in metal chairs
drinking apple juice
near the lilac tress
in Luxembourg Gardens
The infant Gabriel
wriggling in my arms
makes faces
and blows bubbles
as I struggle
to eat a sandwich
At a distance
an indifferent older brother
rides a pulley
six feet off the earth
the length of the playground
And Donna, their mother,
pulls on a jacket
suddenly feeling the chill
of impending dusk
It seems our lives
are strangely out of sync
with this sprawling
patterned and orderly place
Yet our boys peer
beyond the confusion
to something solitary
substantial, maybe

as alive as the sun
that clings to survive
in the sky
at this late hour

# Asleep This Cold Morning

You push your father home
from the hospital
in a wheelchair
along the snowy road
this Christmas morning
Later, he is slumped over
in the chair, the bright
windows behind
silhouette the gray hair
and dark face of sleep
In the other room
the children —
oblivious to this crazy talk
to moments of occasional sharpness —
dance about this cold clear day
assured of selfish joy, their
moment of youth
The old man sleeps
in the explosion of light
afraid only of details
those terribly confusing days
that imprison and keep him
from seeing himself

# Indian Summer Near Temiskaming

*For Robert, Dorothy, Sarah and Alfred*

1

His Christmas card prompted me
to take this train north
certain his wife and children had fled
certain that's what he meant
when he signed only his name
on the Yuletide greetings
Let's face it —
beyond a handful of books on bee keeping
or the 79 uses for goat manure
or eastern religions
he had little to offer in amenities
— no electricity, an outhouse, a goat,
a few chickens, a chainsaw
that refused to start

I find him, there,
at the top of the hill
in a cabin that's outgrown its original size
like a gangling teenager
whose shirtsleeves no longer fit

With him, a daughter and son
the same wife, as ever patient
electricity, a tractor, a half dozen goats
More importantly
the unmistakable aroma
of hot rice pudding on the stove
fresh cinnamon rolls in the oven

2

We step into the cramped chicken coop
where he has accorded names to
each of these creatures
One smaller rooster in particular
he describes as a "back door" boy
for it waits in the shadows
till the other cock is too busy
— or not looking — then rushes about
making much of the moment
This is *Henry* (a.k.a. Henry Miller)
— prolific, sly, above all, patient
As for the hens —
he has christened them
after former wives, girl friends
To them, he confesses, explains,
pontificates, lectures at length
about the wisdom of separation
all the reasons things never work out —
all the time pretending to be so accepting
that someone else now may hold their favor
that, indeed, there may be a legitimate need
to roam freely, to let things be

The truth is, like the women in his life,
these hens seem indifferent, immune to excuses,
to security, to so much good sense

3

His adolescent daughter draws a picture of a deer
and tacks it to the wall in their house —
The doe, with a face calm and confident
swiftly flees the edges of the farm
She pretends it could be her
Later, after she has pulled on coveralls
and gone to milk the goats
squatted down
and meticulously milked each one
— at times squirting milk into a plastic blue dish
for the nearby cat — she decides
it's the sort of gray day in November
a visitor needs some rural entertainment
Or so he says
when he notices his daughter has freed
one of the goats

In muddied large green boots she chases down
the perplexed animal, calling to her, laughing
She doesn't tell her father, but you know
she pretends it's the deer in the picture
darting across the fields running its heart out
so late into this Indian summer

4

It surprises them
how their young son, who barely
can ride a bicycle
has succeeded in riding
one of the goats bareback
When he tells his parents about it
they listen in disbelief
until one afternoon they spy him
through the window
their boy, fallen asleep, arms wrapped
securely around the goat's neck,
the animal prancing happily
beyond the pen toward the bush

It didn't surprise them later
when he confessed to his mother
how once he'd fallen asleep on the goat
and awoke to what seemed more like a dream
— the snow, covering the trees, the sky
awash with stars

5

It is not likely the pictures taken last August
on the blueberry hill two miles away
will turn out
Their young son pried open
the back of the camera
with a fork and exposed the film

Perhaps their reminiscing will suffice —
how she and her mother
scrambled on the rocks
how they mixed berries with rice pudding
brought from home
how they talked
well past chores
regretting never having taken a picture
of a porcupine
how their mother confided
it wasn't far from here
she conceived her
one warm Indian summer day

6

He tells me of the spring
he ran from the house
in stocking feet
how he braced the rifle to follow a hawk
as it sailed low across the open field
carrying away one of his hens
When he fired
the weapon jumped recklessly in his hands
slamming against his face
causing his eyes to tear
He laughs about it now
recalling how his wife had remarked
at that moment that he needn't cry
After all, it was *only* a chicken

*New Liskeard, November 1990*

# Winter In Athens

I

The rain has started in earnest, rolling in
over the gray horizon of the misty Aegean. I
scramble down from the ruins of Poseidon's
Temple, having braced the cold wind to
steal a glance at Lord Byron's signature on
one of the Doric columns.

Later: warming up by the fire at the nearby
café and cupping a hot mug of tea. The sky
a stern chaotic lugubrious soul hovering
above.

Later still: making our way back along the
coast, the bus rolling and meandering its
return to Athens, I overhear a fat lady
complaining how her husband took too long
out there — she had stayed on the bus —
that what he saw couldn't be any different
from those columns at the Parthenon. He
looks away, saying nothing.

Descending twilight — a shepherd leading a
flock down a nearby hill and beyond the
blue-black of the sea is opening up to swal-
low the sky.

**2**

It seems wherever I go this happens — I am
left standing alone and searching for a place
to collect my thoughts, scream or tear out
my hair.

It occurs too often.

*Rome:* Fallen asleep in a taxi. A wide-awake
friend elbows me — "This is the fourth time
we have passed the Coliseum!"

*Istanbul:* I plead with the carpet salesmen for
days to tear up my MasterCard slips and
spend hours on the phone trying to cancel
the transactions.

*Jerusalem:* I leave the city with a collection
of camel whips, skull caps, prayer beads,
chess sets, leather vests, desperately reason-
ing they'll make suitable gifts.

*New York:* Occupying a rainy afternoon,
feeling triumphant I've outwitted a pathetic
salesman ... Only to fly home to find I have
bought four fake Dali paintings.

*Frankfurt:* Stupidly stepping into a bar that is suddenly shut and bolted because the proprietor understood my request for a bottle of champagne meant I wanted a golden-haired fraulein in the corner booth.

*Athens:* It didn't occur to me until I was standing at the centre of Syntagma Square, fuming over the slight of hand trick in a dark little bar that robbed me of $50, that I remembered the cats at the Parthenon scurrying over the marble steps laughing at all the tourists.

3

This morning half way across the world in Athens I recall your remark how it hasn't been long since I've chosen to sleep on the right side of the bed.

I believed I had always done that. Always hugged the right side. Never varied in 20 years of marriage.

You assure me this isn't so. That we've alternated from one side to the other over the years. As casual and natural as steps in a dance. That when I slip my right arm about

you in silent intimate embrace —perfect this
union, perfect this arrangement — in fact
it's been the reverse, a mirrored imaged, an
illusion ... that we actually have faced the
other way for years, that my right was your
left; my left, your right; my face, your face;
your face, mine; and our groping, confused,
paradoxical, full of questions.

I'd always believed the right side was mine.
From childhood when I shared a bed with
an older brother, there I was on the right
side, facing the wall, not the windows, as he
had always wanted. The right side was a
kind of birthright, an unconscious obsession
I'd carried with my body, like a mannerism,
a tic. Over the years we have simply, with-
out bother, faced this way and that, and our
bodies have performed such nocturnal
patterns dutifully, without challenge, with-
out rivalry.

4

My postcards say nothing about the real
things, the things I'd like to let you set free.
You cling to secrets, impressions, *things*.
Once, after you left for a short vacation, I
searched for those treasures ... At the bot

tom of the fridge was something impossible
to identify, something perfectly round,
smooth, liver-spotted. I tossed it away with
so many other things ... In the basement,
there were old skates, coats, unopened
presents, mismatched gloves, a collection of
empty detergent boxes, recipes never tried,
dozens of super 8 film recordings of the
kids' Christmases or birthdays ...

Something about you finds it impossible to
let go, impossible to relinquish ... Maybe I
can only say it here, so far away where
silence takes over the space between us ...

Maybe it's not so awful unless you cling to
secrets, impressions, misgivings, yearnings
... I only hope it won't be too late for me to
grasp ...

5

Barely dawn. Cold drafts from the cab's
window. I ask the driver to shut it but he
chides me suggesting I should feel at home.
This is like England.

The rain pelts the Square as the yellow car
navigates the morning rush hour. All I want
him to do is roll up the window.

This isn't unusual. The days always begin in an argument.

After the window we dispute the price of the ride. Then squabble over the destination. Which airport I should fly out of. Which airline is better. Soon we take on everything else — democracy, the phone system, taxation, the benefits of television, tourism, the English language, soccer ...

"OK, I'll shut the window!" the driver screeches and throws up his hands. Then immediately lights up a cigar. When I point out the sign on the dashboard that states in four languages how smoking is prohibited in the cab, he chortles, "This is a democracy! My vote gives me the right! *You* have no vote here!"

I ask if he'd *please* crack open the window. He does so, ceremoniously, flamboyantly, zealously, proving certain compromises may be possible.

*Athens, November 28, 1989*

# III
# Playing God

# The First Lady
*For Kathleen*

She's been at Gethsemani
for 10 weeks, already
making waves, sporting a
sharp-tongue and severe grimace
as she cleans up in
the kitchen —
the first woman
hired by the monastery in
its 145-year history
She doesn't like
what she sees
*You can tell when*
*there's not a woman*
*around — things just*
*aren't clean like*
*they should be*
stated in that southern
drawl at a long
wooden table
in the bowels
of the monastery
just down from
the refectory
where she serves
the retreatants
She talks and smokes like
there's no tomorrow
doesn't hesitate

to tempt monks
with trying cigarettes —
*Go for it* she taunts
a Latin American priest
who actually accepts one,
rolls and flips it like
he used to as a boy
but reluctantly
returns it to the package
Kathleen's her name,
a Kentuckian who
resides five miles down
the road, someone
they trust — indeed
they're fond of her, not
afraid of asking her
what's the best way to
cut up a chicken,
what she'd cook if suddenly
a bus turned up with
a dozen or more guests
What surprises her is
how the monks
discussed her among
themselves before
hiring her and
agreed she should
work for them

yet she knew nothing
about it — *I hadn't*
*even applied for a*
*job. I'm a housewife*
*and got six kids*
*so I don't need*
*this* —But they
petitioned her husband
a mechanic working
for the monastery for 15 years
to ask if she'd take the job
*It was a hoot, let*
*me tell you and I came in*
*and told them there was some things*
*I was going to do*
*and some things I wouldn't*
*and yesterday gave them all hell*
They'd prepared too
much porridge
and she wound up
having to mop it up when
a novice accidentally dropped
the container on the
floor — *Have you*
*ever tried to mop up oatmeal*
*off a tiled floor. Try it! It'll*
*drive you nuts!*
Beneath the

harsh veneer
Kathleen is more a silent fighter
—maybe even shrewd
or subtle — and everyone here
knows the story, how
fifteen years ago
her eighteen-year-old son,
had left Bardstown
one Halloween night
with his buddies
to raise hell and toss eggs at
houses in the country
and as their car
sped away from
one targeted house
on the outskirts, someone
from the darkness
fired a .22 calibre
rifle and the bullet ricocheted
and exploded in the boy's brain
Kathleen spent the next
five days at the hospital
praying her heart out
and the night her son
died, it was another
son's birthday
When the inquest was over

she didn't battle the police
or the courts — they resigned themselves
to yet another unsolved murder
But she knows, knows his identity,
where he works, what kind of
man he is, where he shops,
where he vacations, what church
he goes to Sundays, and how
many rifles and pistols there
are in his gun case in that house
on the edge of town — she's
made it her business

# The Last Pie

I go down to Sorrento's
on Erie Street
a café that bakes pizza
in large silver ovens
on the other side
of the wall from
a smoky room crammed with
snooker tables
and where the
television roars with
Sunday afternoon soccer games
I watch a swarthy man
slice through a
steaming pizza with
a pair of garden shears
and place each slice
into a cardboard box —
not the sort of
pizza, neat
and triangular,
but irregular
uneven,
Then I drive home
to meet my father
and sister who
have come over
for dinner
Kids everywhere —

hockey nets
baseball bats
toys scattered
across rooms,
the sort of chaos
that makes you
want to walk
right back out
to the car
and drive straight
to Alabama
or some place
with a quiet motel
Instead, you step into
it, smiling because
you know your fate,
nodding to
everyone, breaking
open the box
and letting hands
at the pizza
and it's hard to focus
on anything in
particular, to listen
to anyone for
more than a few
seconds, but
my sister is holding up

something, saying
she's brought
the ginger ale
I nod absent mindedly
with thanks
but she's holding
up something
not a bottle, but a pie
and says it
again, but it's
not ginger ale
she's saying, it's a
pie, a pie that
our mother made
six or eight months
ago — it's been
in the freezer all
that time
It makes me pause
because our mom
died about a month
and a half ago
She'd been in the
hospital, and a day before
she died, had promised
she was going to
make me a pie

You would have to know
my mom, her supreme
optimism, how she believed
in things that couldn't possibly
happen — often didn't —
but persisted in that faith
and there she was dying
and promising to get out
out of the hospital
to bake me a pie
I know it doesn't
make any sense,
but there I am
at the end of August,
a few weeks
from what would be
her birthday
and I'm cutting
into a piece of
that apple pie
It doesn't make any sense
but it makes me wonder
if she was right
all along

# After the Rain

*For all the neighbors*

I

It was a rainy morning in the spring
when we saw the place
Just one walk-through
made us decide to buy it —
a one-room school
at a crossroads of a hamlet
long ago having
sunk into obscurity
A month later
we moved in, discovering
how we hadn't noticed
there was no running water,
no well, indeed, no
hope of one
I didn't find out
the whole story
until seeing old Mister Donais
down the gravel road —
There, sitting in his kitchen
the two of us on rocking chairs
side by side, drinking coffee
He asks, "So what're you going
to do about water?"
"I guess that's why I'm here."
"I can't give you any," he says, flatly.
"I'm supplin' my boys ...

There's only enough for us!
So what'll you do?"
"Guess I'll have to dig a well."
"A well? Where're you goin' to put it?"
"I don't know — What I mean is,
 I'll get a well-digger in, let him decide."
"Nothing to decide —
they've witched it ... There's nothing!
They've dug everywhere
There's nothing. Easier priming a man to
spit."
That's that. We rock back and forth
in the gloom of the kitchen —
listen to the rain on the tin roof
of a nearby shed
I say nothing till Mister Donais speaks:
 "You got a big roof over there!"
At that, we both stop rocking
hunch forward in our chairs
stare out the window at the schoolhouse.
Yup, I say to myself, it's a big roof
but what in hell does that mean?
I just nod, and wait for an explanation,
Hell, hope for one
Instead, he repeats himself:
"Yessir that's one big roof you got!"
I haven't the faintest idea
what he's alluding to
until he gets up to fetch a pipe

then turns to me: "Have you
ever thought of the rain?"
I'm relieved he's changed
the subject, but what the hell,
we've gone from roofs to rain
What does that mean? Is this some
philosophical equation he's testing
me with? I just want water in my house
The old farmer knows he's dealing
with a bone head
"A cistern!" he informs me
then lights his pipe and puffs deeply
Suddenly it all makes sense:
collecting  rain water from the roof
yes, and with that I flee home
finally with all the answers


2


Building the cistern?
Something else again
It was apparent I'd become *entertainment*
for the few scattered families
among the concessions
It's not uncommon for farmers
to pull up by the side of road
to check out the action, the comedy
and naturally they were curious

how I'd get it done
There I was, hiring someone
to build the tank and sink it into the ground
Before digging, he asks where I'd like it
Standing by the side of the house
facing it, watching my young daughter
play at the window, I turn around
and point to the poplar tree near the fence
With that, the well digger swings around,
kind of pushes back the cap on his head
raises an eyebrow, and
asks incredulously, "Over there?"
There being about seventy to eighty feet
from the building
"Yeah, I think so."
He shrugs, and hauls in equipment
to dig the hole and sink the form
then advises me — as did all the neighboring
farmers who had gathered around
the opening in the ground
It'd be best to put in galvanized piping
to link the cistern to the house
"With galvanized, you'll never have trouble
— it'll be there forever.
 You'll never have to dig again!"
I drive into town, ask for eighty feet of
galvanized — it's going
to cost me hundreds of dollars

I return to measure, buy the piping
but wait till dusk to link the well to the
house
then quickly cover the trench
Five years later, I sell the house
move to the city
Another rainy spring morning
when I get a call from the new owners:
"We've checked everything,
and we can't figure out why we're
not getting any water
The pump seems to be working
the well is full and we know it's not
the line, because everybody around here
says you put in galvanized
so it can't be that
What do you suppose it is?"
I blush, feeling as if I'd just been
caught red-handed ... I want to confess
how I'd ignored the warnings — some even
claimed they'd seen me covering up
the line, swore up and down
the line was galvanized, boasted
nothing short of a nuclear war
could destroy it
After a long pause I concede
it's not the pump or anything else
— it's probably the line
I had not used galvanized after all

Instead I buried cheap rubber hosing
Not only that, I'd measured with
a wooden ruler and prayed
for five successive winters
that somehow, somehow
the line would hold, and
nothing would go wrong

# The Affairs of Death

About an hour after
my mother died
I'm on my hands and knees
in the hospital room
scanning the tiled floor
for one of her tiny pearl earrings
I am a boy again
in her bedroom
on Prado Place
that humid summer, 1950,
kneeling there beside her bed
yellow blinds pulled down
my mother yearning to sleep
I can't wake her
I can't wake her
but will she stop sleeping?
There I am this morning
just past dawn, sun barely
wiping its eyes from sleep
my mother's face
far from dreaming
far from all of us now
seeing all
that we can't see
all we fear
I envy that small boy
I'd treasure his control
I can't wake her
I can't wake her

*June 12, 1992*

# Carpet Salesmen

1.

First there was Omar
An hour after my arrival
he leads me
to a tiny shop
in a glut of streets
near the Blue Mosque
A young son arrived
with apple tea
as the father launches
into his sales pitch, plying
carpets, spreading each
out on the floor,
fetching a butane lighter
to burn the fringe,
and let me smell it,
all to prove its authenticity
Showed me letters from Canada
from satisfied customers
even a faded Polaroid shot
of a Saskatoon couple
who bought three last summer
Every now and then
he'd interject prices
undaunted as I wave
each of them off quickly
protesting I want

nothing at all
Thanks for the tea, but
I've got to get going
He yanks a wad of American bills
ceremoniously from his pocket,
waves it above his head
and throws it on the carpeted floor
then stomps on it furiously
Declares this will bring
him good luck, tells me
the price is now cut in half,
that I shouldn't miss the chance
After all, this carpet will
outlast time, my grandmother,
my children, my children's children,
indeed civilization itself
Long after everything has
disappeared, the carpet
bought here in Istanbul
will still be around
I toy with him, asking
"Well, how much *then*
will it cost me?

2.

My first thought
is she's a hooker —

what with the rouge and lipstick,
leather skirt and brazenness
as she saunters over to my
table in this cozy café, asking
if I was looking for
something special
Naturally I'm thinking tits
and ass, at least I'm thinking
that's what she's thinking, but
no, she means leather and carpets
Like everyone else, she's got
her factory, but that's a lie
I tell her I want to finish lunch
Of course, of course, but
moments later she's directing
me down the street to a cramped
basement where they've got
leather jackets half the price
at discount stores in Canada
Again, out comes
the butane lighter singeing
the corners of the jackets
Please, please don't burn
the goddamn jackets —
I'll buy one
Of course, this isn't easy
They want American currency
I protest, asking why

would I pay American
dollars when I'm Canadian
That's just the way things
are done, everyone pays
in American dollars
I ask if Germans and French
pay in American dollars
I'm surprised they fall
so easily into the trap, saying
of course, Europeans don't
because they're not Americans
Well, neither am I,
and tell her if you want me
to buy this jacket,
it'll be Canadian dollars

3

No one is better than Vulcan
the smooth talking owner
of a carpet emporium
He rarely moves from a chair
to show you the goods
in a four-storey building of
this sprawling grimy city
where he's made a fortune in
international sales
A mere turn of the

head, a snap of his fingers
and lean young boys appear,
shouldering carpets, unfurling
them in spacious upstairs rooms
as you feast on tea, pastries,
beer, whatever you wish
Suddenly you're no longer
thinking in terms of hundreds
of dollars but thousands
Suddenly, quite mysteriously,
prices seem reasonable,
and the notion a few days ago
of spending $2500 on what you
casually might have called
"a rug" would and might have
thought of as utter madness
now seems a bargain
Vulcan is merely a  tutor
there to lend you a sense of well being
In that quiet repose,
almost Zen like, he applies
no pressure whatsoever
Hours later, you're still in control
After all, you've got the perfect "out"
But when you announce
how much you'd like to buy the carpet
but need your wife's approval —
and she's in Canada —

Vulcan doesn't blink an eye
A snap of the fingers and something
said in language
you can't fathom
and a boy rushes in
with a telephone
and you witness yourself relinquishing
the numbers of your home phone
and watch Vulcan dial your wife
He greets her with "Hi, this
is Vulcan calling from
Istanbul, your husband's here
and can't decide on the color
of a carpet he's picked out
for you. Can you help?"
Stunned and sheepish, I stutter
to my wife: "Hi, uh, yeah, uhm, yeah,
it's me . . . Ah, yeah . . ."
then fumble to explain my dilemma
Even so, after her approval
I resort to telling Vulcan
I need dinner and time
to consider his wares
He's one step ahead
In an instant, a young boy arrives
bearing steaming trays of food
Saying "No" is fruitless
I buy a $2000 carpet

then leave Vulcan to tackle
my friend who's a little
more eager than I am
After much haggling,
my friend turns to me
and asks which carpet
he should buy
I tell him, pointing out
one in particular I liked
But my friend isn't interested
It's then Vulcan picks up
on the moment, moving
back to me: "Marty, you like this
carpet?"
"Yes," I admit, but protest:
"No, I'm not interested in buying."
Vulcan remains undaunted
"Just give me a price, any price
and it's yours."
I tell him, "Any price? I'd insult
you because I can't afford this!"
"Any price, Marty, any price!"
Okay, I think, I'll give him
a price, a figure so low he couldn't
possibly accept it, and blurt out
"Five hundred dollars!"
With a snap of his fingers
and a few words, two young men
wrap up the carpet.
"It's yours. Take it with you!"

4

They start them early here
The day I depart Istanbul
A scruffy young boy rushes up
Asking me to buy his snake
What will I do?
Play with it
on the plane home?

IV

Tearing Into A Summer Day

# Things That Counted

There were only a few things you had to
keep clear in those days —*Who had the
highest batting average? Who had the lowest
ERA? Who won the Stanley Cup last year?*
I had little trouble with any of these, but
year after year the nuns stumped me with
the first question in the Baltimore
Catechism: *Who is God?* My brother Billy
pulled me aside one day and told me not to
worry — the truth was, he said, I don't
think they know either— that's why they
keep asking.

# Ordinary Man

Everybody's father on the street had fought
in the war ... We'd rifle through closets
and cedar chests for uniforms, medals, shoe
boxes crammed with war photographs of
tanks, concentration camps, armies
marching through cities, fox holes, Nazi
flags being burned ... One friend told us his
father had looted a German barracks,
walked off with Prussian daggers, German
lugers, iron crosses, photographs of Hitler,
the Luftwaffe, you name it ... Another
father had lost his arm in hand-to-hand
combat in the desert with Rommel ... So,
when my friends asked about my father, and
what he'd brought back, I couldn't say he'd
been rejected by the army for health
reasons. I lied. Said he'd been a spy all
through the war. That's why he didn't own
a uniform ... Spies don't wear uniforms ...
For a time he had no identity, carried false
passports, used all sorts of names. After the
war, the government seized all that stuff,
destroyed it ... That wasn't the end of the
lies ... I confided that my father may have
worked at the factory on Seminole, but this
was nothing more than a front for the real
work  He was now engaged in fighting the
Cold War, monitoring the spread of

communism in factories along the border.
Ike telephoned him often . . . In the eyes of
my friends that made my father gigantic on
those idle summer afternoons when he'd
drive home from work, take a beer out to
the verandah, and like any ordinary man
would sit there quietly, reading the paper.

# Leaving My Sins Behind

It was the same every Saturday afternoon
when I was eight — my mother dispatching
us to the matinees with only enough for a
ticket, along with a warning to return home
only once we'd stopped by the church and
gone to confession ... Billy and I would
race from the movies to Our Lady of
Guadeloupe, file into line, tell Father
Mooney how we'd lied, disobeyed our
parents, cheated on tests, and entertained
bad thoughts ...

One Saturday — desperate to go off to the
bathroom — I decided to wait it out in line
for fear of losing my place ... And even
after pushing past the curtain I had to wait
for Billy on the other side to spew out his
sins — probably much the same as mine...

Finally, my turn, and Father Mooney slid
open the panel. In darkness I started: "Bless
me Father, for I have ... " but couldn't
hold it anymore ... feeling that sudden
uncontrollable generous warm wet rush into
my cotton pants ... I started over, sobbing:
"Bless me, Father for I have just peed in
your confessional ..." The kindly
bald-headed priest, straining to make sense

of my desperation, asked gravely, "How
many times  have you done this, my son?"
As if I would make a practice of it . . . In
frustration — trying to stem the flow and
save face —I blurted out, "I'm doing it right
now, Father!" Then fled the confessional
box, holding myself, and scurrying home,
worried sick over how big a sin this was,
how terrible the penance might be, how
many novenas, stations of the cross,
indulgences, rosaries, pilgrimages it would
take for final redemption.

# Natural Acts

I lied about my mother's diamond ring.
I was barely five. . All one long humid
summer morning, peppered with questions
about going into my parents' dresser, about
how I filched my mother's wedding ring,
I finally admitted to it. Knew I hadn't taken
anything. Just got tired of the interrogation.
It occurred if I simply confessed they'd quit
nagging. Instead came a flurry of new
questions, even more urgent: *Where did I put
it? What did I do with it? Where was it?* So I
blurted out the truth. They didn't believe
me. Still more questions: *Why had I told
them that I took it if indeed I had not? Was I
lying?* So I confessed again, owned up to
snatching the ring from my mother's
dresser, to carrying it down to the railway
tracks, to letting a train run over it, to
watching it smash to smithereens. Now it
was gone forever . . . Surely, that would be
the end of it! No: *What train? When did I do
this? Yesterday? This morning? When? Was
there really a train?* Again, I tried telling the
truth. *If it was true I hadn't stolen it, why
would I bring up the railway tracks and the
train?* They didn't believe me. They

believed the lies. Somehow they knew I'd taken it somewhere, hidden it, lost it, fed it to the dog, flushed it down the toilet. I kept insisting on the truth ...

After a while, I no longer knew the truth ... So I'd start all over again, acknowledged stealing the ring ... After a while, I simply didn't know. That evening my mother accidentally stumbled upon the ring, found it wrapped in one of her scented handkerchiefs in a corner cabinet in the kitchen ... It looked like my kind of work.

# Frank's

I learned my first swear words at Frank's.
Words for parts of the body I didn't know I
had. Or thought soon I'd get someday. Or
should. Or prayed I would . . . Body
language . . . In that diner on Wyandotte
men with floppy wool caps ogled the
nyloned curves on the legs of demure
women from the Canadian Imperial Bank
who came in for a coffee ... That's when
I heard those words. After the women left,
the men would talk, guffaw, mutter things
I never understood . . .

Awed by such language, I'd retreat to the
Legion across the street and slump against a
tree in the parking lot and practise the
words . . . Recite them hurriedly like the
Our Fathers and Hail Marys. Silently.
Defiantly. After a while I'd try them out,
ignorant of their meanings, and let them fly
into the wind at passersby . . . Like flipping
open the dictionary to invoke anything
I stumbled upon, then catcalling and derid-
ing anyone getting off the bus or coming out
of the beer store, branding them all "stupid
paleontologists!" or yelling at someone

lurching out of the Legion how I couldn't
tolerate their "onerous face" any longer . . .
Meanings were irrelevant . . . Words gushed
out of me as if I'd been given new power,
new authority . . .

Bewildered by the language, I struggled to
connect these words to something I
understood . . . I couldn't get up my nerve
to ask the men at Frank's . . . One night at
dusk double-riding with Rocky who lived
with his grandmother above Frank's, he let
fly a couple of those words, but didn't know
what they meant either . . . Finally, in
desperation, I asked my mother . . . Her
explanation was so long and convoluted and
boring with exhausting references to
gestation and intercourse and menstruation
and ovaries and sperm and genitalia that I
helped myself to another piece of pie in the
fridge and escaped out the back door,
leaving her there to sit with her tea . . .

# Tearing Into The Street
## On A Summer Day

That day — barely six years old —
I slammed the screen door behind me at
Frank's and rushed into the street and was
hit by a car . . . Only memories are the siren
in the ambulance, later my father at the
hospital, much later the drive home . . .
I lay on the back seat, staring up through
the slant in the back window as we drove
through the neighborhood — the ivy cover-
ing the brick walls of Hiram Walkers, the
lilac, sign posts, cigarette ads flying by and
the blue sky like a blanket limp on the line
. . . Suddenly my father swearing from the
front seat as he wheeled up the driveway
and spotted how — in the space of an after-
noon — my four brothers had constructed a
tree house in one of the maples near the
house . . . My brothers swarmed over the
sides of their slapped-together handiwork,
eager faces and hands greeting my return . .
. As the car came to a halt, the sound of my
father jacking the emergency brake into
place might've obscured what he said as he
leaned out the window to mutter something
to them . . . Not anger, not the usual sort,
or I didn't quite make it out . . . It wasn't

the right moment, I guess .. And when my
father carried me — flopped over his arms
— through the back door, I turned for an
instant and caught the gap-toothed appear-
ance of the picket fence where my brothers
had carefully removed enough slats to build
their house . . .

# The Times Table And The
# T-shirt And The Knife

In the hardware store next to Frank's they
had a Davy Crockett knife, a rubber one,
I couldn't live without . . . All one July,
I planned to steal it because even after I'd
scoured the baseball parks for pop bottles to
cash in, I still didn't have enough . . . The
guilt overwhelmed me for rifling through
the change in my dad's suit pants . . . I was
obsessed with Davy Crockett, knew
everything about him, even taped a picture
of Fess Parker to the wall above my bed,
and spent whole afternoons in the drug store
at the corner, flipping through the comic
book adventures about him . . . I could focus
on nothing else, and when things got so bad
with my arithmetic, and I'd drop my head in
desperation on the kitchen table and plead
with my mother to let me watch Davy
Crockett ... She'd say I could leave as soon
as I got a right answer . . .

Eventually my mother devised the most
abstruse and tangled path to get my brain
around mastering subtractions and additions
and times tables without using my fingers,
all involving Davy Crockett's age at
different times in his life, like when he "kilt
a bar" when he was only three, or when he

started fighting in the Indian wars with
Colonel Jackson . . . And when my mother
posed a equation like, what is 10 times 20,
times six, times four, subtract 3,000 and add
86, because that will tell you the age Davy
Crockett was when he was killed at the
Alamo swinging that musket at the Mexican
invaders . . . I'd swiftly shoot back at her
the answer like I knew what I was talking
about, "Well, that would be 200, then times
six would make it 1200 and times four would
make it 4800 and subtract 3000 would make
it 1800 and add 86 would make Davy
Crockett 54 . . .But if she asked me straight
out what 86 times 54 was, or even something
simple like four times three, I was beaten,
lost . . . There had to be a story, something
that mattered . . . It's still that way . . .

As for the knife, I didn't have to steal it . . .
My mother bought it for me, along with a
T-shirt. Certainly, not for scoring the
highest mark in arithmetic that June — just
for passing it, just for scraping by.

# Sunday Visitor

All of us wanted to be priests. Five sons. All
altar boys. Raised on the border. Assisted at
mass. Memorized Latin. Marched in May
Day "Mary" parades. Made novenas. Went
on retreats. Recited thousands of rosaries...
No wonder make-shift altars sprang up
throughout the house. And Billy and I — no
more than 12 — regularly said mass in an
upstairs bedroom. Inveigling (and coaching)
a younger sister to make routine confessions
to us ... So carried away once in "playing
mass' we swiped the oil cloth from the
kitchen table, turned it inside out, painted
a broad cross on it, and transformed it into
a liturgical vestment ...

One brother nearly made it to the priest-
hood, but dropped out of the seminary.
Another went to work for the bank.
Another became a cop. Another a security
guard ... And I started writing for a
newspaper ... The one we thought would
make it stopped going to mass altogether ...
Each Sunday after mass, he'd comb through
the Sunday Visitor, and address countless
letters to monastic orders telling them how
sincere he was about joining ... And my
father — all one hot summer, 1956 —

slumped in a dining room chair, wearily
fended off Resurrectionists, Capushions,
Franciscans, Redemptiorists, Basilians,
Christian Brothers . . . And sadly confessed
how his son had absolutely no desire for
religious life, how the boy fanned his hair
into a ducktail, drove a hot rod, stayed out
all night, and might soon set the record for
failing Grade 12 more times than any high
school student in the province.

# The Barber Shop

Saturday mornings at the barber shop on
Wyandotte — heads bowed, absorbed in
comic books, waiting our turn on the broad
window ledge or in upright chrome and
leather covered chairs . . . We'd tear out
coupons, truly believing we'd get rich, or
fatten our biceps, become recording stars . . .
Haircuts, always the same: buzz cuts for
summer, trims for winter. There was that
moment of elation when we graduated from
the painted board across the arm rests of the
barber's chair to the soft cracked leather seat
. . . The talk in the place: boring, adult,
male, Korea, trials at Nuremberg, Ike's golf
game, trade of Rocky Colovito to the
Tigers, the Sputnik . . . It was easy to lose
yourself in the multicoloured bottles atop
shelves near the mirror behind the barber,
absorbed in the pungent odor of hair tonics
wafting up like the smell of a new scribbler
in September. . .

That was the '50s when you dreamed of
sideburns . . . Once I actually took my
mom's eyebrow pencil and sculpted wide-
slanting strips down my cheeks, certain no
one would think they were fake . . .
Thought I even had the same lips as Elvis

and stood endlessly in the mirror studying
the trademark sneer. . . . Saturday mornings
we lived imaginary lives as the bow-tied
barber's scissors  fanned over our heads.
Sure, we did stupid things We dreamed
stupid things. Then again, so did everyone.

# House Painter

Maybe my father had the right idea — after
a series of heart attacks, he went on
disability from the plant where he mobilized
assembly-lines, and took up painting. The
doctors believed it would relax him, give
him a sense of well-being.

Today my father does lakes ... Lines up
small canvasses across the expansive pool
table in the basement. Fifteen in a row. And
painstakingly paints fifteen northern lakes.
All the same. When he's finished he climbs
the stairs for lunch, like the days when he
used to drive home from the factory, and
my mother waited with hot soup.

Today, as before, my father's secure in
knowing that upon descending to the
basement awaiting him will be the task of
fifteen cabins nestled among fifteen scenes
of fifteen birch trees. All done exactly the
same. Fifteen times... Tomorrow he'll start
on fifteen sailboats on fifteen lakes.

# Will

Across the room, in the cramped cubicles of
his desk were all the bank statements,
insurance policies, receipts, a miscellany of
papers, including how one of seven sons had
bilked him for more than $7,134.56 in 1965.
He'd co-signed some loans and warned my
brother he'd be left out of the will. Beside
the bed was a K-mart note pad, gigantic
letters in a black magic marker, as much as
an inch and a half high, resembling a
kindergarten kid's attempts at printing their
name ... Though legally blind, he refused
to relinquish old habits, still wrote every-
thing down, clinging to the necessity of
being in control.

In the hospital, struggling to beat back the
pain from the tumors on his spine, he'd
grimace, roll over on his side, tell you he
damn well wasn't going to die, pause, then
ask, humbly "Am I going to die?" Wouldn't
wait for the answer. Grappled for the
transistor radio, searched for it under his
pillow ... Frustrated, he finally ordered one
of us to set it up. He'd already taped over
the dial to lock in CKLW, so we couldn't

screw it up . . . He needed the reports on the
Canadian dollar . . . Wondered if he should
sell what he had . . .

After the funeral, we discovered he'd
known all along he was going to die. On the
note pad by the bed he'd meticulously
itemized the details of his funeral, down to
the choice of casket, the wake. One page
he'd scrawled simply, "Worms;" on another
"Alone." The final page — an outline for the
homily, setting out clearly what should be
said about him . . . He must've had a change
of heart in those moments alone. . . He'd
listed "Patience" among his virtues . . . It
was crossed out.

# Walking in
# Thomas Merton's Boots

*For Brother Anthony*

The field outside the hermitage is soggy
with January rain rendering my street shoes
useless and so I reach for a pair of rubber
boots by the door only to find three
left-fitting galoshes, one right. Someone's
walked off with two rights or so it would
appear. What's with this place?
Everything's labeled *Merton's Water,*
*Merton's Gloves, Merton's Ax.* Everything
else must be mine. Who is this Merton? A
question he probably needed to answer
himself . . . It occurs to me as I push my feet
into the rubber boots and step out into the
dampness leaving behind two lefts that
Merton's out there somewhere — walking
around with two right-fitting boots marked
legibly *Merton's Boots.*

# V
# Autobiographies

# Lies

1.  Naturally I'm not always right.
    Naturally at times I only see one
    side of things. Naturally I'll
    consider changing.

2.  Admittedly I get angry. Admittedly
    I say things I don't mean.
    Admittedly I regret them.

3.  Certainly I respect you. Certainly
    I believe what you say. Certainly I
    trust you.

4.  Of course you're always right. Of
    course I'm not just saying that. Of
    course I believe you.

# Le Zoo

In the WC this morning
it would appear from the patterns
on the floor
that Miro had stolen
the design
revolutionized art

In the street
a young woman sits cross-legged
on the folded-down tailgate of a
truck—
a friend paints a mustache
on her face

Nothing is so magical
as two-year-old Stéphane
fallen asleep after having lined up
all the animal crackers
on a blue blanket

one by one
rhinos, elephants, bears, monkeys
march in single file
along the
Seine

*Paris, September 1985*

# Rhubarb Pie in the Summer Kitchen

*For James Reaney*

It was easy to write
about him, riding
out there with a rhubarb pie
on the back of a bicycle
to the farmhouse
The tin roof calling out
in the afternoon heat
I expected him
to be at the screen door
waving to me from the yard
I expected the black dog
running from the children
who played on the truck tire
swinging from the tired maple
that yielded obediently
at each new demand
It was easy to write about him
because we would walk
out to the pond
ringed by the trees he planted
years ago and by the memories
of a childhood I'd read about
in his poems and plays
I thought it entirely appropriate
to bring the pie
I thought it entirely appropriate
that later we would sit

in the summer kitchen
for tea, that our voices
would wend their way through
the old house, and breathe
there a moment, tucked
away among the crumbling eaves

# Moons Dancing
# In Stillness

Checking the calendar: full moon
    quarter moon
        new moon

Checking out the birthdays of my
children:

*Elise:* Jan. 15, full moon,
dazzling and bursting, contented to sit
and peer down
over scarred maples near her window

and she, satisfied to sit at an old
Royal typewriter
or to bend back the covers
of my favorite books

— the moon, yawning and bored at
such indifference

*André:* Sept. 19, sliver  of the moon
like a skate blade
turning on a frozen pond sheltered
and ringed by poplars

recall perching him on a snow bank
to rest while I cleared the ice
— this two year old yearning to skate

Later, my frozen fingers tying up his
skates

*Stéphane:* Oct. 22, new moon,
its beautiful halo high
over the River Main in Frankfurt
I run, carrying him over one shoulder
through windy rainy streets

Another moment: Stéphane digging
down into a corduroy pocket to pull out
broken lifesavers — joy at holding in
the flat of a tiny hand a constellation of
quarter moons

Those perfect days
Full moon
    quarter moon
        new moon

moons dancing in stillness
before my children
    dancing
    dancing
    dancing

# The Believable Body

When
you give
it gives

Wherever you touch
it touches back

And against your body
it feels
like your body

# Nude Bride

I leave the nude bride
She is asleep
Leave her
a clock on the mantel
a drawing
dishes to do